The Evolution Of Canine Social Behaviour

D1533470

The Evolution Of Canine Social Behaviour

Roger Abrantes

Wakan Tanka Publishers

Published by Wakan Tanka Publishers, Naperville, Illinois, USA
Printed by Distinctive Printing & Graphics, Naperville, Illinois

1st edition 1997

Typeset in Times 11 pt at Lupus Forlag. Printed and bound in the USA.

Contents

The Evolution Of Canine Social Behaviour—Roger Abrantes

'The only justification for our concepts and systems of concepts is that they serve to represent the complex of our experiences; beyond this they have no legitimacy'—Albert Einstein.

Foreword

This book has only been possible thanks to the work of many scientists to whom I wish to pay tribute; I will kindly ask readers to study the bibliography at the end. Their efforts and the research conducted since 1984 at the Etologisk Institute, Høng Agriculture School, Denmark, under my supervision, support the topics presented below.

Behaviour means *the way of acting*. Behaviour *is 'the actions or reactions of persons or things under given circumstances.'*[1] Behaviour means *'conduct, actions bearing, comportment'*. Everything in the way you or I, or our dogs, appear to one another is behaviour. The ultimate purpose of all behaviour is to cope with the necessities of the organism. Behaviour has no existence *per se*, no purpose in itself—it serves other goals. It is therefore frequently difficult to uncover the reasons and motives for behaviour. We can only understand specific displays by comparing the unknown traits of one species with the known patterns of another. This comparative method often proves rewarding and is a significant tool for the study of behaviour. Comparison means discovering not only similarities, but also differences. The former are useful in supporting new ideas and subsequent studies, but the latter are also fruitful, often answering the original question and raising new quests at the same time.

To observe objectively, without a single preconception, is impossible and remains nothing but a theoretical issue, a testimony of our incapacity to comply with our own standards. Problems arise with the very first question: to observe, yes, but what? The choice of what to observe is a restriction, the first breach to be crossed in order to comply with the rule of objectivity. Any journey of discovery needs a preconceived map, and mine is no exception.

Of all the scientists whose work has contributed to this book, I believe the classic ethologists, and particularly Konrad Lorenz, influenced me most. John Maynard Smith and Richard Dawkins's theoretical issues, together with the field work of David Mech and Erik Zimen have also affected my thoughts. However, they bear no responsibility for my application of their observations and theories, nor for any errors I may have committed.

I am indebted to my English editor Sarah Whitehead, for her editorial work. Thanks also to the staff of the Etologisk Institute, especially Dr Birkes Poulsen for their valuable suggestions and contributions.

Solbjerg, December 1996

Roger Abrantes

1. The strategy of life

There is only one objective: to live long, and preferably long enough to pass half of one's genes to the next generation. This is the ultimate and universal goal for all living beings on this planet. There are as many strategies for achieving this objective as there are living forms. We have uncovered many of them, yet biologists occasionally discover new species. There is only one correct strategy in life: to prolong life and to postpone its extinction; death.

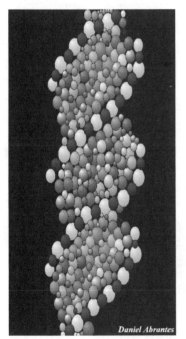

Daniel Abrantes

DNA Strands

Nucleic acids are complex molecules produced by living cells and are essential to all living organisms. These acids govern the body's development and specific characteristics by providing hereditary information and triggering the production of proteins within the body.

Computer drawing by Daniel Abrantes.

Life is the activity of all organisms, from primitive forms such as blue-green algae, to complex ones like mammals. This activity falls into two major categories: metabolism and reproduction.

Metabolism is the physical and chemical processes by which the organism uses energy from its environment for self-preservation. The energy source can be heat, from the sun, for example, or the chemical energy of ingested food. A living organism converts energy.

Molecules called *nucleic acids* control reproduction. *Deoxyribonucleic acid* (DNA) molecules can make copies of themselves. They are what one organism gives another. Reproduction involves making copies of the cell and results in copies of the organism itself, except in the case of viruses, which have a completely different strategy.

Life probably originated very early in the history of the earth when a sort of *replicator* somehow occurred. External sources of energy powered this primordial replicator that could make copies of itself. The first replicators eventually evolved into cells. Natural selection favoured the replicating molecules that could find energy most promptly, and evolution took care of the rest: procaryotes, nucleated cells, multicellular organisms, plants and animals. Evolutionary success depends on the ability of an organism to preserve its genes.

It is impossible to give a precise and general definition of life. I shall, nonetheless, attempt this feat, since in this study I will not use an idea without a prior definition.

In a crude sense, we can say that an organism is alive if its *metabolism* and *reproduction* are operative. Death implies, in complex living forms, the cessation of heartbeat, respiration, movement, reflexes and brain activity. Everything threatening one or more of these functions is threatening to life.

Red Fox, Vuples vulpes - *Red foxes tend to live near farmland, which provides them with good hunting ground and plenty of rodents.*

Life **is the unique characteristic of an organism when its metabolism and reproduction are operative.**

There is never a single rewarding strategy for the organisms that exist in any given environment. The wild canids of the Serengeti offer a good example. The hunting dogs, *Lycaon pictus*, follow the herds of gnus, *Connochaetes*, to feed the pack and their youngsters. The jackals, *Canis aureus*, on the other hand, stay in the same territory. They survive the drought by consuming any edible thing they can find. It is a desperate hunt for energy and yet they succeed. During this period the jackal hunts alone to sustain itself and its small family.

The wild canids of the Serengeti have found two different, but equally successful strategies in the same environment. One selected the strategy of staying together in large packs, persecuting prey and hunting it down. This dramatically affected the spectrum of behaviour shown by the species, resulting in a larger range of communication patterns than the jackal. Jackals

Jackal, Canis aureus - *Jackals form remarkably long-lasting pair bonds. Males enforce this monogamy by chasing off any suitors whose presence threatens the survival of their progeny. A jackal pair raises a litter together. A pup from a previous litter may remain with the family as a helper and protector.*

live in well-defined groups with few conflicts, because there are only two adults—one of each sex—plus one yearling and three or four pups. They do not need more than a limited repertoire of signals.

Nothing in life is free and nothing is free of consequences. No one has ever formulated these principles as such in a scientific context, and yet they express a basic truth. Life is an exchange of one sort of energy for another. Hunting dog and jackal interact with their environment, and their behaviour, social or not, is invariably the best available strategy in the given circumstances.

There is, however, a third strategy. Widespread in the meadows and grasslands of Europe we find the continent's most common canine hunter, the fox, *Vulpes vulpes*. Also known as the red fox, it chose the strategy of loneliness. Alone after dusk, the vixen hunts for herself and for her young hidden somewhere nearby. Foxes do not have complex communication patterns—they simply do not need them. To communicate presupposes a receiver, and the fox wanders alone in woods and copses. The behaviour of the fox reflects its strategy of life, as does the behaviour of the hunting dog and the jackal.

Many wild canids once lived in North America. The wolf, *Canis lupus*, and the coyote, *Canis latrans*, survived—partly because of human attempts to save the survivors of the once abundant fauna on this part of the earth. A cousin of these canids, the red wolf, *Canis rufus*, was not so fortunate and is now close to extinction. *Canis rufus* did not prosper because it never discovered the right strategy. Whether the wolf would still exist without human intervention is another question. It may have survived in the inauspicious northern parts of the American continent—unless the whole species had become a victim of an epidemic catastrophe.

Strategies for living are many and varied. The 'preservation of favoured races in the struggle for life'[2] happens according to numerous plans. In the family of canids alone, we find three distinct strategies:

1 - Solitary predators.
2 - Family pack hunters.
3 - Large pack hunters.

Communication patterns increase from 1 to 3. Being social has a price. For some it pays off, for others it does not. Foxes resolve encounters with conspecifics using displays ruled by aggression or fear: attack, defence and flight.

Jackals are a bit different and difficult to classify. The same mechanisms

Gray Wolf, Canis Lupus lupus - The gray wolf, also called the timber wolf, is distributed across northern North America and Eurasia. It is found in a variety of habitats including mountains, plains, deserts, forests and tundra. The wolf is a social canid and lives in packs og 4-16 individuals.

seen in the fox rule most encounters, but sometimes their behaviour assumes radically different measures—as for instance when a yearling female in the pack begins courting a strange male. The parents clearly show their disapproval and yet the yearling neither attacks them nor flees. The jackal shows a compromise behaviour that we have become accustomed to call submission.

It is by observing the large pack hunters, like the wolf and our dog, *Canis lupus familiaris*, that we realise there is more to communication than aggression and fear. The experienced observer has no doubt that the mechanisms ruling the wolf pack's rendezvous are distinctly different from those governing the encounter between two foxes in the sparse light of a winter moon. Initially, this difference was described by saying they show fear-aggression, without the realisation that no creature can ever show fear and aggression simultaneously. Sometimes human terms are used, by saying that they show dominance and submission, without the full realisation of the implications of these terms. However, this barely matters—at this point the confusion in terminology is already too extensive to make any difference.

So let us start from the beginning. What makes a social animal special is its ability to compromise, to win and lose and still get the best possible out of each situation. This means to apply mechanisms other than the great motivators, fear and aggression.

Fear and anger, the fight for survival, the ability to find food or sexual partners, alliances with other species and so forth, are traits we find in many different animals of many different species. Some of them will be adept at coping with individuals of the same species. They need their conspecifics to survive and selection has favoured those among them who were best at co-operating. Time turned them into true champions in the art of compromise. Their secret is that they seldom exercise fear and aggression in social contexts. Instead, they have discovered other mechanisms with which to deal with relentless conspecifics.

Each individual's original task was: 'to fulfil my will, without killing or harming the other fellow, who I need for my survival and that of my offspring.' Evolution treated this like any other task, and time contributed to perfect the amazing ability of *social self-awareness*. The result was obvious. The social individual developed two states of social self-awareness: *self-confidence* and its opposite, *insecurity*.

The social organism is thus an expert in solving social puzzles. It masters the application of *fear* and *aggression*, as well as behaviour motivated by what we shall now call *social awareness*.

Among these champions of compromise we find wolves, horses, chimpanzees, humans, and their best friends, dogs.

2. In the beginning...

A new-born puppy looks helpless. It cannot see and yet it can find its mother's teats and suckle. It does not hear very well and it has not yet developed a good sense of smell, yet it will whine and wail when separated from its siblings, when it is cold and lonely and until its mother carries it back to safety. There are no signs of the great mechanisms of social self-awareness that will turn it into a specialist in its field. At this early age the puppy, in common with all other new-born creatures, concentrates all its energy into survival.

Life arises from warmth and moisture. The new-born puppy is a living example of this principle. Warmth and milk are the two most pressing necessities and the female gives them freely. There is no need for aggression

Wolf cub enjoying life and the warm sun—keeping its metabolism operative!

and even fear does not express itself fully. Only physically unpleasant or painful experiences, such as cold or loud sounds, trigger fear.

However, all too soon fear will make its entrance in the young pup's cognitive world and with it will bring aggression and then submission and dominance—or whatever we choose to call it!

Coyote (Canis Latrans) - The coyote is the most widespread canid in North America: from Panama northward to the North Slope of Alaska. Coyotes can survive in a variety of habitats and have successfully adapted to an urban existence in many parts of the United States and Mexico. Essentially nocturnal, coyotes feed on carrion, small rodents, birds, insects, snakes, lizards, and even deer and sheep.

3. Motivation

There is great confusion, not only in popular literature, but also among scholars, over the definitions of some concepts used to explain behaviour.

In the past there have been two opposing theories as to what behaviour is: either animals learn everything, or they know what to do instinctively. In more recent times, scientists have built models explaining behaviour by combining elements of both. My own suggestion, which I use in defining all concepts in this book, falls into this category.

The most predominant school in explaining behaviour has been *Behaviorism* (J. B. Watson and B. F. Skinner)[3]. Strict behaviourists assume that all behaviour is learned and formed through *conditioning*.

At the end of the last century, Russian Ivan Pavlov[4] discovered classical conditioning, and then in the beginning of the 20th century American B. F. Skinner clarified the rules *of operant conditioning*. To an orthodox behaviourist, animals must learn all behavioural patterns by means of trial and error. Extreme behaviourists also apply this rule to human behaviour.

There is, however, a completely different way to account for behaviour. *Ethology*, developed in Europe at the beginning of the century, assumes that much of what animals know is innate and performed instinctively. The genes programme entire behavioural sequences. Extreme ethologists maintain that all new behaviour results from *maturation* or *imprinting*.

The Nobel Prize-winning founders of Ethology, Konrad Lorenz, Nikolaas Tinbergen and Karl von Frisch[5], uncovered four strategies by which the genes programme behaviour: *sign-stimuli* or *releasers*, *motor programmes*, *motivation* or *drives* and *learning*, including *imprinting*.

Sign stimuli or *releasers* are signals that enable an animal to recognise a vital item, or another living creature, when it discovers them for the first time. We can easily detect sign-stimuli in communication, hunting, and fear-elicited behaviour.

Motor programmes account for the display of another type of behaviour. The first studied motor programme was in the greylag goose, *Anser anser*: the egg-rolling response. When a goose sees an egg or something that resembles an egg outside its nest, it stretches its neck until its bill reaches it, then gently rolls the egg back into the nest. Such a behaviour is a fixed-action pattern and ethologists maintain that it is innate.

An *instinct* is innate programming to perform a complex behavioural sequence without prior learning. Instinctive behaviour patterns are usually responses to specific stimuli such as patterns of feeding, mating, parenting and aggression. In each species instinctive behaviour develops according to natural selection. Instinctive behaviour helps an animal to save energy in its personal ecological niche.

There is, however, another class of motor programmes beside instincts. They are the learned patterns, like walking and swimming, that animals perform unconsciously after a time.

A central idea to understanding behaviour is *motivation*. *Motivation* is what compels an animal to do what it does. When we define the idea as such, motivation does not seem to be worth deeper study. However, the task of the scientist is more difficult than first assumed. It consists of observing the animal's behaviour and changes in behaviour, without intervention from subjective factors, preconceived assumptions or theories.

We must thus define *motivation* exclusively with the law of causality: *every effect has a cause*. But what are the causes? At first, we may answer by saying that what motivates the animal are *drives*: self-preservation motivates hunting, sex motivates mating and aggression motivates the expulsion of a rival.

However, the problem is more complex when we become aware that drives operate through an intricate system comprising of many behaviour patterns, some of which are inborn, while others develop through interactions with the environment. In the end, we are left with a new problem: what is a *drive*?

A *drive* is a force, an urge onward, a basic need, a compulsive energy. I do not think we can find a more precise definition. The English language uses the word *drive* with a huge number of different meanings such as, *'move, propel, push, shove, thrust, herd, stab, pilot, impress, plunge, strain.'* Basic abstract ideas such as, *'a cause to move, a forcible penetration, a readiness to engage energy'*, are common uses of *drive.*

Scientists do not accept one single theory of motivation, but a general tendency is apparent. Some psychologists have been keen to stress that motivation aims at reducing stimulation to its lowest possible level. Thus, an organism seeks the behaviour most likely to cause a state of *no stimulation.* Recent theories of motivation, however, picture humans seeking to *optimise,* rather than minimise, stimulation. These theories account for exploratory behaviour, variety-seeking behaviour and curiosity.

It was the classic school of ethology founded by Konrad Lorenz that first explained behaviour by means of *drives* and *motivation[6]*. There are alternatives, of course. B*ehaviourism* is one, as we have seen. Another alternative is to explain behaviour in evolutionary terms, as Maynard Smith and Richard Dawkins have done.[7]

However, we must remember that scientific models are just our way of trying to understand matters of fact, our environment and our place in it. *'Reality is independent... of what you or I or any finite number of men may think about it,'* to put it in the words of Charles Sanders Peirce[8]. Models are successful if they attain specific goals and have a practical use. Beyond that, they have no value whatsoever, although I am not sure everyone would agree.

In my suggestion of how to explain behaviour, I employ the ideas of *drive* and *motivation* defined in terms of the smallest possible entities, probably the *gene*. I have not found any need to go beyond the gene, although another scientist might find this rewarding.

I picture the interactions between all entities, from gene to complex organism, as a whole. Specific laws regulate the dynamics of interactions towards *an evolutionarily stable strategy,* as we will see in due course.

In my view, models built at different stages during our scientific discovery do not necessarily express different matters—nor for that sake different opinions—only different approaches. I see no incompatibility between parts of Lorenz and Dawkins's work, or even more blatantly between the behavioural and the ethological approach. Up to a certain point, it all depends on the level at which we study our subject-matter.

I do not think we can do without *motivation,* partially because this is a common idea in our way of thinking. If the idea was damaging I would discard it without mercy, as I have done with other ideas, such as fear-aggression and dominance-aggression.

The concept of motivation is highly relevant to communication patterns. There is no behaviour without motivation. Most of the dog's facial expressions and body postures are motivated by fear, aggression, dominance/superiority and/or submission/inferiority as we shall see. Motivation is also very decisive when teaching the dog various tricks or exercises.

Henceforth, in my crusade to clean up the mess of terms in the behavioural sciences, I will not use a term or notion without a preceding definition. Thus we define motivation and drive as follows:

Motivation is what compels an animal to do what it does.

A _drive_ is a force, an urge onwards, a basic need, a compulsive energy.

4. Fear

Fear[9]
1. Fear is a feeling of agitation and anxiety caused by the presence or imminence of danger.
2. A state marked by this feeling.
3. Reverence or awe, as towards a deity.
4. A reason for dread or apprehension.

In the popular mind, fear is an unpleasant emotion; the expectation or the awareness of danger or pain causes fear. It is also agitation or dismay in the anticipation or presence of danger. The two definitions say the same, only the first sees it from a psychological perspective and the second from a behavioural one. The interesting point is that we use the word fear interchangeably with both meanings, yet we know little or nothing about the inner state of animals' minds.

The third definition is also interesting. It implies a notion that fear may be something other than a behaviour elicited by danger. It also suggests that we may mistakenly call *reverence* fear, which is an attractive explanation of certain behaviour patterns in social animals.

What we call fear is a stress reaction to anything considered dangerous.

The hawk-goose display—an innate reaction of fear.

This silhouette resembles a hawk and a goose depending on in which direction it is moved. An experiment showed that ducklings and goslings reacted with fear to the hawk display and ignored the goose display.

Drawing by Daniel Abrantes.

The popular view upholds this. Fear is also having *cold feet, agitation, trepidation*—all with physiological implications.

Fear elicits a series of physiological and anatomical processes aimed at the best possible solution for survival. For a puppy there are several available alternatives, such as retreat, whine, or lie down and yelp. All these are typical patterns of behaviour elicited by fear. Fear usually leads to flight or immobility and sometimes to displacement behaviour.

Fear is probably innate, for it is vital to the survival of the individual. Without fear, no individual survives long enough to be able to reproduce itself and pass its non-fearful genes to its offspring. The first time the new-born shows fear-elicited behaviour depends greatly on species-typical behaviour. Maturation happens at very different rates and there is no point in comparing a child, a pup or a duckling. However, if fear behaviour usually means flight, immobility, and/or vocal distress, there are some common features between different species.

A silhouette resembling a hawk, *Accipitridae*, when moved at a certain speed above the nests of goslings, *Anatidae,* elicits fear behaviour when moved in one direction, but not in the other. Hawks have short necks and long tails, while flying geese have long necks and short tails. The experiment suggests that some animals have an innate image of danger and are therefore able to show fear behaviour without previous learning.

We can therefore ask whether fear behaviour is a question of innate responses to sign-stimuli or programmed learning. Most young learn vital information immediately after birth from direct interaction with one or both parents. Young ducks must follow their parents from their first day of life. As in many other species, a duckling must quickly learn to identify its parents. Evolution has attained this feat of memory by compelling ducklings to follow the first moving object they see, and that coincides with a species-specific departure call. The call is a sign-stimulus, but it is the act of following which triggers the learning.

This primary parental-imprinting phase happens early and is brief, often ending 36 hours after birth. Fear behaviour may evolve in a similar pattern. There is an initial pre-programming to flee, freeze or express vocal distress to certain stimuli, but young have to learn these stimuli.

It is very important to identify a parent among numerous conspecifics as well as identifying life-threatening factors. It is likely that the young uses all its energy to sustain life. We saw earlier that the infant needs warmth and food. Its genes strongly pre-programme it to seek them. However, these are to no avail if the organism is defenceless. Effective defence systems must develop soon after birth.

The most rewarding strategy is a combination of a pre-programmed mapping, with confirmation of the programming immediately after birth, on the first occasion where the organism is in a situation of potential threat from the environment. The influence of the environment immediately after the birth and its everlasting effect is what we call *imprinting*.

A few minutes after hatching, we can easily pick up a duckling and hold it in our hands. Only 24 hours later, the duckling will try to run away unless we have imprinted it to us. In those vital 24 hours the duckling has learned to react defensively to the presence of a threatening stimulus.

Experiments with wolf cubs, *Canis lupus*, show that although this period of imprinting is longer than in ducks and most birds, it is just as important. Holding a wolf cub in our hands for three minutes a day in the first 10 days makes all the difference in its behaviour towards humans later in life.[10] The same applies to our domestic dogs, *Canis lupus familiaris*, even if it is more flexible. The difference is that we have selected dogs for thousands of years for their sociability. We may assume that they have many genes determining this trait, which allows imprinting for longer, or over several periods. Birds are among many animals which experience several rounds of imprinting. After the first imprinting to vital matters, another round, or rounds, usually take place. These serve to define the species image the individual will use to select an appropriate mate when it matures.

Lorenz found out that *sign-stimuli* determine the fixed action patterns of a species in a specific environment. He showed that such patterns are as important a part of an animal's self-preservation mechanisms as its physiological traits, and that they had a similar evolutionary development.

My assumption is therefore that, as the world became over-populated, the role of sign-stimuli in some animals shifted from identifying each animal's threatening stimuli, to guiding the learning necessary to distinguish between them. This strategy works because, at an early age, most animals' contact is limited to their parents. Most parents, having invested half their genes and huge amounts of energy in their offspring, are pre-programmed to show protective behaviour towards their infants. Through this behaviour they teach the young what to fear and what not to fear. A mistake in identifying life threatening stimuli is thus highly unlikely.

Immediately after birth, fear is connected to unpleasant physical stimuli. Later, it follows a general pattern in the development of the puppy, and other stimuli will elicit fear. To learn about what is unpleasant or dangerous is a vital exercise. The unpleasant constitutes a danger for the welfare of the organism and the danger is unpleasant.

We can offer different explanations for this, of course. We can say that the unpleasant motivates the puppy to act to minimise or optimise its stimulation—the psychological trend. We can also say that unpleasant experiences demand energy and all organisms are pre-programmed to save energy. Solving an unpleasant situation releases energy for more vital activities—the ethologic trend.

As fear leads to *flight, immobility, vocal distress* or *displacement activity,* it is important for the individual to be able to display the most purposeful behaviour in each situation. It is vital to react to fear-eliciting stimuli, i.e. danger, in an almost reflexive way. Animals of many species, especially those which live in constant potential danger, like prey, show that a good flight mechanism saves lives.

Immobility must be convincing enough to eliminate danger. Of course, it is no use to be so fearful that one forgets how to swim when carried by the stream towards the rapids! For a sitting grouse hen, however, total immobility is the best available strategy if only a few yards away from a sneaking fox. Fleeing would mean the loss of all her eggs.

Another profitable display of immobility is in certain confrontations with stronger conspecifics. This behaviour is the best strategy for the puppy, as there is no chance they can fight back.

Soon enough though, another great mechanism will begin to govern the puppy's reactions. As it physically matures, other alternatives arise, and fighting back becomes an option.

Before we look as these options, let us define the ideas we have studied so far.

Fear is the drive that motivates the organism to react to an incoming threat.

A *threat* is everything that may harm, inflict pain or injury to the individual or decrease or oppress its chances of survival.

Fear elicits flight, immobility or distress behaviour.

5. Aggression

Aggression[11]
1. The initiation of unprovoked hostilities.
2. The launching of attacks.
3. Hostile behaviour

At about four to five weeks of age puppies begin to show the first signs of aggressive behaviour. They engage in conflicts, they even seek them, and they are undoubtedly more assertive. They are also more aware of the world around them and more conscious of themselves; they are constantly looking for challenges. Unquestionably, their motivation does not seek to minimise stimulation, but optimise it.

The first confrontations appear to arise by themselves. Although there is food and attention for all, competition for resources usually triggers conflict. These are not fights about the items themselves, because the puppies have no interest in possessing things. Disputes arise perhaps simply because the pups are together; or in more philosophical terms, because they happen to be in the same place at the same time.

At this stage, the pups begin showing aggression in a way we would usually understand it. Indeed they *initiate unprovoked hostilities* and they *launch attacks* on their siblings. If *hostile* behaviour means *unfriendly* behaviour, and if *unfriendly* behaviour is the opposite of *friendly*, that is *amicable, pleasant, agreeable, favourable, enjoyable*, then they surely display hostile behaviour.

The problem with the popular understanding of aggression is that it is not applicable for other encounters, although undoubtedly the same forces motivate them. If we can say that the aggressive behaviour of a puppy is unprovoked, only a couple of weeks later all puppies will be constantly provoking, which is another word for challenging, all the others. Their behaviour is the same, only more refined since the puppies have matured.

The problem is, as Lorenz showed in 1963,[12] that aggression, in the popular mind, is only half the truth. We repress the other half because our ethics say that it is wrong *to be aggressive.* There is a great difference between being aggressive and *showing aggressive* behaviour; and again there is a big step from showing unprovoked aggressive behaviour and *after a provocation.* Not that it makes any difference from an epistemological or biologic point of view. None of these disciplines care for what is right or wrong. However, in common speech, we use the word aggressive with negative connotations. We say *'he is very aggressive and she is not,'* which is wrong. If both *he* and *she* are humans, *Homo sapiens sapiens,* then both are aggressive creatures. What we should say is *'he often shows aggressive behaviour and she seldom does.'*

The first disputes between pups are very similar to those seen in solitary or non-social predators like the fox. At this state of their development pups or wolf cubs are not yet social animals. To be social means to *become* social.

All new-born animals are selfish. We can take this is a definition. When they grow up they may lose some of this egoism, and become social. We are presumably the most sophisticated social animals, even if ants and bees live in amazingly complex societies. We invented a word to describe a very peculiar form of being social: *altruism.* It means *unselfish concern for the welfare of others.*

The idea of *altruism* is interesting and may give us a cue to understanding the true nature of being social and why aggression is necessary to be social. In a crude sense, showing altruistic behaviour means to exhibit selfish behaviour in a more sophisticated form—not in the pursuit of immediate advantage, but of long-term benefit. To behave like this means to be social. How this happens is another question. My guess is that it has to be learned, but it can only be learned where there is a genetic disposition for it. It is in this way that most traits, behavioural or not, develop into phenotypic traits. Certain coat colours in canids and other animals do not show at birth, but develop later. Social behaviour could have the same gene-anatomy.

In a society of bees, *Hymenoptera apidae*, workers strive continually in the hive for three weeks, after which they emerge and forage outside until they die two or three weeks later, totally exhausted. They leave no offspring.

The altruism of honeybee workers has a genetic explanation as we shall see. In a population of honeybees, genes favouring assistance in rearing the

Honeybee, Apis Melifera—As they fly from flower to flower, worker honeybees collect pollen grains in a special basket located on the hind leg. Pollen, the main food source of protein, vitamins, minerals, and fat, is necessary to the development of queen, worker, and drone. Field bees place pollen directly in the cells of developing larvae when they return to the hive, where they also regurgitate nectar for its conversion into honey.

next generation of sisters offer a better strategy than a traditional own-off-spring-strategy.

Kin selection, uncovered by W. D. Hamilton[13] is widespread. An animal performs certain services for the benefit of relatives. The honeybee is the ultimate example, because of the genetic benefits. Kin selection also operates in other animal communities. Male lions co-operating in taking over another male's pride are usually brothers. Female lions in the pride hunting together are sisters, daughters and aunts.

We, *Homo sapiens,* are also subject to kin selection. Anthropologists have unveiled many so-called simple cultures organised along the lines of kinship. Our stone-age ancestor, who hunted in the grasslands of a recently ice-freed Europe, lived in societies based on kin selection programmes.

Altruism is sometimes a mutual-aid system. Chimpanzees, *Pan troglodytes,* groom each other, removing parasites from areas they could not reach by themselves. This mechanism is central to human societies. This is the 'I help you now, you help me later'—principle. Such a system requires that an animal is able to recognise another as an individual. For the system to work properly, those who accept favours without paying them back must be rejected. This is a valuable cue to understanding the anatomy of social behaviour.

For social behaviour to operate as a stable system, it has either to induce a great genetic benefit, or a short-term benefit of the type 'I favour you now, you repay me later.' The latter only works because the individuals are able to recognise one another. Observations show that the more aggressive a species is, the more easily individuals recognise each other. It is mainly among highly aggressive animals such as wolves, dogs, chimpanzees, geese and... humans, that we observe so-called personal relationships. Honeybees, although highly social and altruistic due to their sophisticated genetics, neither know each other individually, nor do they show comparable levels of aggression.

After five weeks, puppies will take issue over possession of items and food. Confrontations are initially confined to siblings. They are harmless and the puppies suffer no injury. They are not disputing resources. They have the luxury of being able to optimise their stimulation and they show curiosity towards everything in their path. If they meet an animal of a species that later will be their prey, they treat it like any other object of their curiosity. Prey is not food, for food is what you get from your parents and eventually other adults. They cannot connect *parts* of the prey, especially well-regurgitated parts, with the animal itself. Investigating their future prey in this way allows invaluable information to be gathered. Learning is the keyword, and the basis of this special genetic programme.

The only conflicts in this period of the pups' life are with siblings. Competition, the cause of conflicts, is thus what elicits aggressive behaviour.

There are still some issues left for our present study before we offer our final verdict on aggression. However, to order our thoughts so far, we shall attempt a definition of aggression. Then we shall analyse it thoroughly.

> • Aggression is the ability to show aggressive behaviour, to attack.
> •Aggression is a drive triggered by competition, usually by a conspecific.
> •Aggressive behaviour aims at resolving or assisting conflicts.

Aggressive behaviour is predominantly motivated by the appearance of a conspecific, because they are the fiercest competitors for the same basic resources.

We observe fighting between conspecifics in practically all vertebrate species. Fish nip each other; birds attack one another; horses bite and kick; cats scratch and bite each other; rats kick and bite; sheep butt their heads together. They fight as their genes have programmed them to. They fight because they have very similar needs and find themselves in direct competition over food, mates, and dwelling spaces.

Chimpanzees are known as intelligent communicators and problem solvers. They prepare and use a wide variety of tools such as long, peeled digging sticks, grass stems, sponges and rags. They may use these tools for enlarging the holes of insect dens, pulling termites or ants out of their nest mounds, or smashing the harder-shelled of the 20 kinds of fruit they often eat in a day. Males also use sticks and rocks in their charging displays. The chimpanzee differs from man by only 1 percent of its genetic material and is our closest relative.

How much, how long and how fiercely they will fight depends on the final weighting of risks compared to the benefits. Male sea elephants, *Mirounga leonina*, will fight to the death over possession of the harem because defeat is equal to genetic suicide. Male elks, *Alces alces*, on the other hand, engage in pushing contests with their antlers. The one that becomes tired first retreats with the expectation that next year's mating season may bring better results. The idea of the fight is not to stab, wound or kill; antlers are shed at the end of the mating season.

Wolves and dogs have similar strategies. Males may fight fiercely, yet they do not usually harm each other with their powerful jaws and teeth, although mishaps do sometimes occur.

Most intraspecific aggression happens in this way. It does not result in significant bodily harm, especially in social animals, where the weighting of the pros and cons of having to live with conspecifics falls in favour of the social benefits.

Identification is an important aspect in the mechanism of aggression: the more one opponent resembles another, the stronger a competitor he probably is. This is probably acquired as a sign-stimulus during the time when pups begin fighting with one another. They all look alike and they all compete over the same things. Later in life, resemblance will act as a sign-stimulus for aggressive behaviour, or the potential for it, as we shall see. It will obviously also act as sign-stimulus for other relationships as well, especially in social animals.

Animals sometimes direct aggressive behaviour towards members of another species. The triggering cause is still the same, competition or danger to the organism. Or is it? Are there really two types of aggression: (1) interspecific aggression, the conflict between members of different species; and (2) intraspecific aggression toward conspecifics?

Some modern *companion animal behaviourists* (not to be confused with the original behaviourists) divide intraspecific aggression into: (1) *competitive aggression*, and (2) *defensive aggression*. Interspecific aggression can, in their view, also be seen as *predatory aggression*.

Competitive aggression is the result of different species competing over the same resources such as food or water. This is not unusual in certain environments. Hunting dogs, *Lycaon pictus*, and jackals, *Canis aureus,* may compete over the odd carcass. Jackals often have to fight hooded vultures, *Necrosyrtes monachus*, to consume the rotten carcass of an unfortunate Thomson's gazelle, *Gazella thomsoni.*

Lions, *Pantera leo*, and spotted hyenas, *Crocuta crocuta*, are known as the fiercest rivals. They fight mercilessly whenever their paths cross. They do not give their rivals a chance to flee or surrender, they go straight for the kill. They do not treat members of other species much differently from the way they treat their own. Lions and hyenas are both highly aggressive animals living in a form of society. Their levels of aggression combined with the rudimentary mechanisms of dominance and submission result in a high mortality rate within their group. A lion or a hyena can never feel safe, as they are commonly killed by their own pack-mates. The price for being aggressive and social is high, but evolution can obviously afford to pay it.

Usually though, competition is more fierce between individuals of the

The male northern elephant seal typically weighs more than three times the female seal. Territorial and polygamous, these male seals battle for females and for prime locations on their breeding beaches.

same species, and fiercest of all between animals of the same sex and age, according to the principle of resemblance.

In theory however, there is no difference between interspecific and intraspecific aggression when induced by competition. There is therefore no need to create a new term. Competition triggers aggressive behaviour; it does not make any difference which *object* causes it.

Defensive aggression is the behaviour of the animal under attack—a sort of retaliation. The comments which apply to *competitive aggression* also apply to this type of aggression. Aggression is always defensive in one sense or another.

Predatory aggression, towards prey, aims at obtaining food, which is not compatible with the definition of aggression. It does not make any sense to speak of aggression *towards a source of energy*—food. Defenders of the term predatory aggression add that 'this type of aggression characteristically does not involve emotions such as anger and can be considered as a component of feeding and subsistence behaviour.' This is the same as saying that predatory aggression is not aggression, but they failed to find a better name for it.

Aggressive behaviour is under constant development, in parallel with the physical and motor development of the pup. There are three crucial circumstances to explain the ontogeny of aggression: (1) competition with siblings, (2) weaning, and (3) the father (supposing they live in a normal pack).

First there is the odd bone. Puppies meet the urge for aggression for the first time over trivial items. They fight with each other and, without knowing it, they are having their first lessons in how to become social animals. Soon, they realise that they cannot handle siblings by means of aggression and fear and then other strategies begin to appear.

All this happens simultaneously with their mother denying them the best and cheapest source of energy they ever will have, suckling. The time where goods are free is coming to an end, all too prematurely in their minds. Every time they see their mother they try to suckle and sometimes, if they join forces and catch her by surprise, they succeed. Perhaps this is the first sign of active co-operation among puppies. Alone they have no chance. The mother will seize them by the nose, pin them to the ground, growl at them and they will run away, whining and howling.

At roughly the same time they meet their father, or another adult male member of the pack for the first time. It is usually the first association they have with a complete stranger. Until then, they have only met their mother and siblings. Initially, the father is tolerant and complaisant. Then the first conflict occurs. He is tender but also strong and awe inspiring. No doubt the puppies fear him at first. They run away whining, as they did from their mother during weaning. Then suddenly, they seem to change strategy.

This is a crucial period in the development of the pup's social behaviour. The role of the adult members of the pack, especially the mother and father, cannot be over-emphasised. Learned experience is an important determinant of aggressive behaviour in canids as well as in humans. Elicitors of aggression are learned. Repetitions of aggressive behaviour are more likely whenever it is successful.

In our domestic environment, pups of 8-12 weeks old are likely to exchange the dog pack for a human pack, and at this time they may learn, as children do, that aggression can enable them to control resources. Children learn aggression by observing others behaving aggressively, but it is unknown whether dogs do the same. It has been proved that children whose parents discipline them with physical force tend to use more physical aggression when interacting with others. Research also shows that pups disciplined by tough males, show tough behaviour more often than others brought up by a benevolent male.

We can now settle for a definition of aggression.

Aggression **is a drive directed towards the elimination of competition.**

Aggression is necessary to protect the organism and to allow it to perform its main task: metabolism and reproduction, or in other words, to live.

Everybody competes for a place under the sun: food, sexual partners and territory, undoubtedly the three most important resources for most organisms. Like fear, aggression is a reaction to a potentially endangering situation. An opponent is always a danger unless you control him or her totally.

Adult male lions can be as much as 50 percent larger than females. Their manes make them appear bigger without adding expensive weight. If a smaller male realizes he is at a disadvantage, a confrontation may end without a fight. In the event of an attack, the mane also serves to snag or cushion the impact of an opponent's claws and teeth.

6. Limiting aggression

Fighting involves a certain amount of risk and can lead to serious injury, or even death. Evolution therefore shows a tendency towards developing mechanisms which restrain the intensity of aggressive behaviour.

One of these mechanisms is a genetically programmed tendency to establish *territories*. There is no reason for an animal to expand its living or foraging area, if sufficient resources are available for themselves and other members of their family group. Hence conflicts normally occur as border scuffles. However, controlling a territory may become an issue of crucial importance.

Males typically compete for territories, either fighting actual battles or performing ritual combats as tests of strength. This is probably an evolutionary purposeful distribution of labour. Females *generate* the offspring, either by laying an egg or carrying the young inside their bodies; males take care of appropriate nesting sites to maximise the chances of the offspring's survival. Weaker males may be excluded from keeping a territory or be forced to occupy less desirable sites. If they attract a female the chances of the survival of their offspring will be smaller. Territorial fights have therefore a selective effect on the population.

Territoriality serves as a mechanism to distribute resources favouring the fittest, and to limit the reproduction of those that are less fit. Wynne-Edwards[14] argued that the sacrifice of excluded animals was for the good of the group and species; *group selection* evolved for the cumulative genetic good of the species. This theory pointed out the difficulties that evolutionary theory had in accounting for *altruistic* behaviour. It sparked the theories of *kin selection*, and *the selfish gene*,[15] where evolution acts on individuals rather than on groups.

The *ritualisation* of aggressive behaviour is another genetically programmed restraint on combat, as Lorenz proved. Bulls, *Bos primigenius taurus*, scrape

Hyenas, Crocuta crocuta, are well adapted to both scavenging and hunting. The hyena is an equally intimidating hunter, capable of bringing down a wildebeest many times its own weight after a chase reaching 60 km/h (37 mph) and covering 5 km (3 mi).

the ground with their hoofs; lizards, *Squamata*, expand a skin fold in their throat; horses, *Equus Caballus*, lower their heads and flatten their ears; chimpanzees shake branches and shout; wolves and dogs snarl and assume a corpulent appearance.

The advantage of the ritualisation of aggressive behaviour is that all parties save energy. All have something to lose in a conflict and everything is a question of the mathematics of energy and the probabilities of survival. The winner has much to lose if it becomes exhausted as a result of a fight; the loser has the advantage of living to see another day and another chance to win. An injured winner may not defeat the next opponent and may become vulnerable to predation.

Most species have clear signals that indicate acceptance of defeat which terminate combat before injury occurs. The lizard *Squamata*, crouches, while a tropical freshwater fish, the cichlid *Persiformes cichlidaé*, retracts its fins.

The dog lies down, exposing its unprotected throat and belly, and the gull, *Charadriiformes laridae*, offers the vulnerable part of the back of its neck to its adversary. Horses clap their teeth, an appeasement gesture commonly seen in foals.

Each of these behavioural traits signals acceptance of defeat and immediately halts subsequent aggression. This takes place in many species in various forms and the more social the species, the more refined the mechanisms become. Among the species with extremely well-developed aggression inhibiting mechanisms are the dog, and its ancestor the wolf.

Two six-week-old puppies play. They tumble around and bite one another. Suddenly one of them has a grip on the other's ear. It bites hard and the poor brother or sister howls in pain. Fortunately for their ears, roles reverse from time to time. With its ear firmly grasped, the puppy succeeds in getting its teeth in the tender skin of its sibling's belly. Much whining and yelling follow. They stand still for a short while, let go, and then just look puzzled.

Next time they act slightly differently. One will grasp the other's ear only until the puppy begins making noise. It will react to the sibling's vocal distress, which works as a mechanism to inhibit or control aggressive behaviour. Previous experiences showed the puppy it is better to let go at the first signs of vocal distress, or its belly will hurt. This is learning by trial and error.

Another situation: the female chews a bone. The puppy wanders up. She gives a warning growl. The puppy ignores it and continues towards the bone. Ten inches from the bone the mother jumps like a flash, seizes the puppy by the muzzle and pins it to the ground. The pup whines and then runs away. Ten minutes later the same situation arises. This time, the mother growls and the puppy immediately comes to a halt. It licks the air with its tongue, twisting its hind leg out to the side and waving one front paw. This is what we call *pacifying behaviour* because it has the effect of ceasing the opponent's aggressive behaviour.

Pacifying behavioural traits are patterns previously used for other functions. All these functions have an aspect of pleasure in common. The puppy is displaying the same movements that used to bring the good things of life. The licking is associated with suckling, the leg twist with the mother licking its belly and the pawing with the stimulation of milk production. And it all works! The mother will continue chewing her bone and the puppy can run away safely.

The pup has learned another important lesson: how to deal with stronger,

When an adult herring gull, Larus argentatus, returns to the nest, the chicks pecks at the red dot on the end of the large beak to obtain the food it may or may not carry. Yet it will just as eagerly peck at the red eraser on the end of a pencil. This instinctive blind response is a fixed action pattern and its trigger (the red dot) a sign stimulus, or releaser.

aggressive conspecifics. Although totally unaware, the pup has had its first lesson in ritualised behaviour.

A third situation: the wolf cubs come out of the den. They see the alpha male, probably their father, 10-15 yards away. They run to him and nuzzle him, trying to lick his lips and simultaneously performing the characteristic leg twist. They flop down in front of him, belly up, and then quickly stand up again to follow him and repeat the whole procedure. The father growls slightly. After some time he will seize them by the muzzle, as their mother did during weaning. They lie down voluntarily when he grasps them. Then, satisfied, they will leave the old male in peace, running off to play with one another or a yearling wolf.

These three typical situations show us that there is more to the understanding of social behaviour than aggression, fear and the simple control of both by territorialism and ritualisation.

Is the puppy who bites its sibling and causes pain just mean or stupid? Is the female teaching her offspring the meaning of aggression? Is the male teaching his offspring the meaning of fear? Why does ritualised behaviour work?

The question of cruelty or stupidity we can disregard without much attention. Stupidity— being slow to learn—is heavily punished by the laws of selection. If cruelty means to inflict pain, than life is thoroughly cruel. If by cruelty we understand the act of inflicting pain for its own purpose, then the concept does not belong to the realm of ethology.

The pup continues to bite its sibling in spite of its expression of pain. Either it does not know it is inflicting pain on the other, or doesn't appreciate the possible consequences. It learns this through its own pain when its sibling's teeth grab its belly. Whether it realises what pain means to the other is irrelevant. What matters is that it learns to act in response to the other pup's message of pain, and stops biting.

It does not make sense for the female to be aggressive towards her defenceless offspring. First she invests 50 per cent of her genes in each one, then she carries them inside her body giving them vital resources she needed for herself. Then she gives birth and protects them from the dangers of the environment. Why should the female suddenly become aggressive towards them? If she injures them and they die, she loses 50 per cent of her genes for each pup and the whole endeavour, conception, pregnancy, parturition, lactation, has been a terrible waste of time and energy.

When her pups have become adult and compete with her over the same resources, she may have an advantage in being aggressive, but not when they barely can stand up.

The answer can only be that the purpose of maternal behaviour is not to teach the cubs to be aggressive, but how to avoid aggression. The purpose of her behaviour is to prepare the cubs for their future lives in the pack. Experiments show that pups who grow up without contact with other pups or adult dogs never learn the full repertoire of social behaviour.

The female teaches her offspring how to compromise—how to survive when 'you get your own way, and when you do not.'

To recognise sign-stimuli is the most important task for the infant immediately after birth. It saves its life. Compromise is the most important lesson a social youngster may learn after having learned fundamental life-saving sign-stimuli. It maintains the fitness of the social life of the pack. Selection has proved this, as it favours individuals that develop behaviour enabling them to stay together. Other animals, the solitary predators, do not need these social traits. These organisms found other ways of dealing with the maintenance of their metabolism and reproduction.

The male wolf does not teach the cubs to fear him.[16] If this was the case, the cubs would run away from him instead of towards him. Why do they keep following him and bothering him? They need food and protection from him. Ideally, they want him to regurgitate some food, but if this is not possible they will go for acceptance. It is interesting that these two behavioural traits are so closely linked.

The puppies follow the male, jump up and try to lick his lips. Sometimes they lie down, exposing their bellies. They show conflicting behaviour motivated by two desires: to come closer, and to flee. Either the male regurgitates food for them or grasps them by the muzzle. Either way, the pups are satisfied. Food is always good, but second best is if the male grasps them without hurting them. This gives them security—as they learn it will also happen next time. They will then dare to come forward again in the pursuit of an easy meal.

Thus, the cub's begging behaviour has two consequences: it provides food and acceptance. For a social animal, genetically programmed to seek company, acceptance is not a bad strategy from the selfish gene. It is energy saving!

In simple terms, the puppies want the male to demonstrate that he accepts them and will not harm them. It is an exercise in self-control which they provoke him to use—'show us that you can grab us with your formidable jaws without harming us. Show us your self-control. Show us that we can feel safe with you.' A male can fail this exercise in two ways: either by ignoring them, or by hurting them. An adult which ignores puppies is a waste of energy for the young: no food, no contact. A violent adult is life threatening.

Learning to be social means learning to compromise. To compromise means to get what you want sometimes, but not at other times. It also means 'I'll do you a favour now, you repay me later.' It means 'I won't kill you now, because I cannot hunt alone.'

Social animals spend vast amount of time together and conflicts are inevitable. It is therefore sensible for them to develop mechanisms with which they can deal with hostilities. Limiting aggressive and fearful behaviour by means of inhibition and ritualisation is only partially safe. The more social the animal is, the more effective mechanisms are obligatory. Inhibited aggression is still aggression; it is playing with fire on a windy day. It works well for less social or less aggressive animals, but highly social and aggressive animals require other mechanisms.

Of course, I cannot prove this point conclusively, but I can demonstrate that it is highly probable. In the long run it would be too dangerous and too exhausting to constantly recur to the great drives to solve banal problems. Animals under constant threat, or constantly needing to attack others, show signs of pathological stress after a time. This suggests that social predators need mechanisms other than aggression and fear to solve social animosities. This applies even to other animals besides the social predators, such as the horse.

It is my suggestion that social animals, through the ontogeny of aggression and fear, develop two other motivational factors. If the meaning of aggression is 'go away, drop dead, never bother me again', the meaning of *social-aggression* is 'go away, but not too far, or too long.' Equally, *social-fear* says 'I won't bother you if you do not hurt me,' while *existential-fear* does not allow any compromise—'It's you or me.'

The significant difference between the two types of aggressive behaviour seems to be the motivation. If a wolf pack comes across a strange wolf in its territory, it will chase it unmercifully and will probably kill it. Observations in North America show that many wolves lose their lives this way. If the individual is a pack member however, they will meet and probably show displays of ritualised aggressive behaviour. There is a significant difference in motivation depending on whether the opponent is an *alien* or a *mate*. Aggression deals with the *alien* and social-aggression with the *mate*. Equally, fear and social-fear deal with alien and mate.

It is the change in motivation that leads us to the creation of these two new concepts. Social-aggression and social-fear show conflict behaviour. There is nothing spectacular about that, since we know that ritualised behaviour arises from conflicting behaviour. Appeasement behaviour shows conflicting intentions. As an example, the wolf cub alternately increases and decreases its distance from the alpha male. More importantly, ritualisations often involve a change in motivation.

A classical example of a change in motivation is the courtship behaviour of some species of bird. Females beg from their mates using a posture found only in juveniles soliciting food from their parents. This happens during a restricted period of the breeding cycle—the females are not hungry.

Another classical example is the courtship behaviour of the green heron, *Butorides viscerensis,* which has been studied in great detail. The male chooses a nest site and defends it with a characteristic call, warning other males. Intruders are threatened by *a forward display*. The male's call attracts females, but they do not dare approach because of the *forward display* of the male. They persevere, however, and the males' behaviour progressively changes. A *snap display*, where the male shows ritualised nest-material gathering, finally signals acceptance. The *stretch display* is a ritualised form of flight, and is common in many birds. The *stretch display*, the direct opposite of the *forward display*, signals non-aggression. The *snap* and *stretch displays* gradually give way to displays where male and female fly around together. It is only after the *contact displays,* mutual billing and much preening, that copulation takes place.

Courtship behaviour in dogs and wolves is very similar. Initially, the female shows aggression. The male reacts with juvenile behaviour such as *play-face* and *play-bow*. Then it is the turn of the female to show displays of juvenile behaviour. Next, both dogs *wrestle* for a while and it is only then that the female allows the male to make a tentative mounting. After much tussling, the female allows the male to mount her without moving away.

In the process of ritualisation, behaviour displays change because motivation changes. The signals lose their original function and gain a new meaning.

It is therefore tempting to say *that motivation aggression* changes into *motivation social-aggression*, or *dominance,* as we shall see later, when two *mates* meet. Equally, *motivation fear* changes to motivation *social-fear*, or *submission* as we also shall see.

For the time being we shall call the two new motivators (1) social-aggression and (2) social-fear.

Social-aggression **is a drive directed to the elimination of competition from a mate.**

Mates **are two or more animals, which live together and depend on each other for surviving.**

Aliens **are two animals which do not live together and do not depend on one another for survival.**

Social-fear **is the drive that motivates the organism to react to a threat from a mate.**

A *social-threat* is everything that may cause submissive behaviour or flight in an individual, without harm, pain or injury occurring

Social-fear usually elicits submission in response to the other's threat or flight.

Lone wolf looking for a 'mate.' Wolves are very social with strong bonds between them. 'Mates' are two or more of these animals, which live together and depend on each other for surviving.

7. Social aggression and fear

While all populations are unique in some way, it is possible to describe general characteristics. Isolation tends to cause a population to develop locally useful traits through natural selection. If the isolation persists, selection and eventual mutations may lead to the appearance of a new species. Members of this new species may not be likely, or even able, to interbreed with the species from which they originally derived.

It is conceivable that the first social predators originated in this way. Changes in the environment may have favoured the members of a certain population which were able to solve intraspecific problems by means of less aggression and fear than most part of their counterparts. A fashionable trait soon spreads in the population. Whether social-aggression and social-fear appeared solely as a product of evolution, or were helped by some favourable mutation, we do not know. It matters little in this context.

The newly-created genetic mapping for social-aggression and social-fear is built on the recognition of sign-stimuli. It involves a disposition to recognise certain signals and display certain behaviour patterns. This is, of course, dependent on the environment and on learning processes.

From the very first time a pup stops biting its sibling when it shows vocal distress, it has learned to react to a specific sign-stimulus. This happens at a certain age because genetic mapping dictates it.

Next on line is the alpha female, the mother. She attacks the puppy, but it quickly discovers that by lying down and staying still it suffers no harm, pain or injury—in short, the attack is under control. Lying down, pawing, etc. are used because they have previously had pleasant connotations. Certainly, these actions initially had other effects, but for the pup this is of no concern. The curious thing is that the same behaviour still works. Now the pup knows how to control the female's attack, and very soon all the other adult member of the pack, too. In fact, the pup seems to try out its new skill deliberately with the alpha male, and it works.

Meanwhile, the pup is also exercising its new ability to control another's retreat without needing to bite. Rehearsals take place with one sibling after the other. The pup experiments by growling, snarling, etc. Occasionally, things go wrong—as they sometimes do in life—but the puppy knows how to cope. Lie down and it will go away. A brief scare is not discouraging, on the contrary, it adds another dimension to the game. All this time, the puppy is learning to be a social predator, to be one in a world of many, where sometimes one has to give way in order to win in the end.

Social-aggression and social-fear deal with situations *here and now*. They motivate the individual to use certain displays with the purpose of reaching a well-defined goal. The aim of social-aggression is to exercise most influence or control, to have first priority. Therefore we shall call it *dominance*. Indeed, the term *dominance* already exists to explain the social organisation of some groups of animals.

Dominance[17]
1. Exercise of most influence or control.
2. Most prominent.
Dominance is supremacy, ascendancy, pre-eminency.

Social-fear, on the other hand, aims at solving a threatening situation by surrendering. We shall therefore call it *submission*—another term already used to explain animal behaviour.

Submission[17]
1. To yield or surrender oneself to the will or authority of another.
2. To allow oneself to be subjected to something.
Submission means: surrender, concession, giving in.

From this point onwards, I shall only operate with the four main motivators of social behaviour to explain all agonistic interactions. The four motivators of social behaviour in social canids are:

> *Aggression* **is a drive directed to the elimination of competition.**

> *Fear* **is the drive that motivates the individual to react to a threat.**

> *Dominance* **is a drive directed towards the elimination of competition from a mate.**

> *Submission* **is the drive that motivates the individual to react to a threat by a mate.**

8. Dominance

The wapiti, or American elk, although originally ranging throughout the temperate regions of North America, is now largely restricted to mountainous areas of the United States and Canada. Wapiti herds migrate with the seasons, moving in the spring from lowland areas to mountainous areas where they remain until the late fall, when they again return to lower elevations.

Dominance is a term widely used to explain animal as well as human behaviour. As we have seen, dominance is social-aggression, which does not aim to destroy the competitor, but control it.

Dominance usually relates to a high status. Dominant individuals have a high status or rank, and a subordinate a low status or rank. The terms *rank* and *hierarchy* are therefore used to explain social interactions in a pack of dogs or wolves.

A rank order, consisting of dominance-submission relationships, was first observed in domestic fowl, *Gallus gallus domesticus*, in which dominant individuals tend to peck subordinate individuals. Hence the reason for the term *pecking order* being sometimes used interchangeably with *rank order*.

A relevant feature of the pecking-order is that members learn to recognise one another individually, provided they live in a stable flock. Dominant individuals are more able to use their rank to gain priority over resources, such as food, mating partners and roosting sites.

Dominance-submission relationships are widespread in the animal kingdom, and have certain features in common in many species. In dogs, they are for the most part originally formed in aggressive disputes. If one wins a fight, then the combat may not happen on subsequent occasions, instead the defeated individual is likely to show immediate submission. This depends on the ability to identify individuals within the pack. It is for this reason that Lorenz claimed aggression is a necessary premise for the creation of individual bonds.[18] The more aggressive an animal is, the more vital it is to recognise other group members in order to be able to show due submission when necessary.

How many encounters are necessary to establish a dominance-submission relationship depends on many factors: (1) species, (2) the individuals, (3) available resources, (3) the constitution of the group and (4) the environment.

Some species, or even breeds, are more aggressive than others. Cocks of some breeds of domestic fowl need only a couple of encounters to establish a stable rank order. Others never do and may fight to the death. The same applies to domestic dogs where individuals of some breeds usually settle for next best, rather than risking serious injury.

Resources play a decisive role as well. If there is enough food, the number of agonistic encounters fall drastically.

The optimum ratio of males to females in a group also varies from species to species. In domestic fowl, a predominance of males seems to work well, while in kennels, one male dog and several females is usually more harmonious. Curiously enough, zoos find it easier to keep wolf packs with more males than females.

It is incorrect to assume that once a dominance-submission relationship is established there are no further displays of aggression. This is not the case for either domestic fowl or canids.

Hierarchies work because a subordinate will often move away, showing typical pacifying behaviour, without any obvious signs of fear. Thus, the dominant animal may simply displace a subordinate when feeding or at a

A subordinate wolf will often move away, showing typical pacifying behaviour, without any obvious signs of fear. Thus, the dominant animal may simply displace a subordinate when feeding or at a desirable site. Hierarchies in nature are often very subtle, being difficult for an observer to uncover.

desirable site. Hierarchies in nature are often very subtle, being difficult for an observer to uncover, as Mech experienced with the wolves of Isle Royale[19]. The reason for this subtlety is the *raison d'être* of dominance-submission itself: the subordinate animal generally avoids encounters, although the dominant one is not too keen on running into skirmishes either.

Dominance-submission relationships are established by learning. Some species show immediate outward signs of dominance. In domestic fowl, dominant males are normally larger and have a more prominent comb than subordinates, but the opposite also occurs. Hormones affect the anatomical signs of dominance, which in turn affect the animal's rank. For example, female dogs oppressed by a very dominant alpha female may not come into heat at all.

In many social species the dominant males mate most successfully. Zimen[20] unveiled an interesting feature: even when the alpha male is not responsible for the majority of copulations during the mating season, he is, more often than not, the father of most cubs. In an observation of elephant seals, *Mirounga occidentalis*, the most dominant six per cent of the bulls inseminated 88 per cent of the females.

The genetic contribution of dominant males is so great that it is surprising that subordinate characteristics survive in the population. The problem is that as the numbers of dominant genes increase in the population, the subordinate genes begin to have an advantage, as Dawkins showed.[21] In the end, the ratios between the dominant and the subordinate genes settle into a *evolutionarily stable system* (ESS), where a certain amount of both genes create stability.

Some species, however, solve the problem without gene intervention. In red deer, or American elk, *Cerves elaphus*, the dominant males are so busy maintaining their rank that subordinates often have a chance to sneak in and mate with a female. This is also observed in large wolf packs where the dominant male is constantly challenged.

A third strategy concerns the high mortality rate amongst rival dominant males, enabling subordinate males to improve their rank. In some species this strategy assumes extreme consequences. Male red deer fight frequently and do not eat during the rut. If they do not die of exhaustion in combat, they will probably die during the following winter.

The strategy of submission is wise. Instead of vainly engaging in a desperate fight, waiting may prove to be much more rewarding. By employing appeasement and submissive behaviour, subordinates are often able to shadow dominant animals and profit from opportunities to gain access to vital resources. By showing submission, they also gain advantages from the membership of the group—particularly defence against rivals. This is vital for a species chased by predators and useful for social predators, where the possession of a territory may mean survival.

In some species, immature and subordinate males may detach themselves from the group. Subordinate male lions, *Panthera leo*, leave the pride. Male and female wolves leave the pack spontaneously, or after remaining in the periphery for a while.

Some species have hierarchies dependent upon location. Wolves do not because each pack has one territory. However, a domestic dog's rank may depend on the distance of the meeting site from its home territory or feeding area. This is common between dogs that know one another well and pair together to investigate their environment. Woodchucks, *Marmota monax,* and octopus, *Octopus cyanea*, show similar mechanisms. This system requires individual recognition, a feature that is crucial for the development of the dominance-submission relationship.

When recognition is not possible, as for instance in Canada geese, *Bransa canadensis,* stable dominance-submission relationships, i.e. hierarchies, do not form. Consequently, there are more displays of aggression and fighting. Canada geese cannot be highly social in the same way as wolves because they lack one important and indispensable ability: to be able to recognise one another.

However, such animals limit the number of combats by means of a *rule* for the outcome of encounters, corresponding to the following order: parents with young, paired adults, yearlings in families, single adults, unattached yearlings. In spite of total ignorance about *game theory* and *mathematics*, the societies of Canada geese show an amazing consistency with the rules of these disciplines.

Even if such a strict pre-established outcome of encounters does not take place in dogs, aspects of it do relate to their ordering. The construction of such a rule for dogs could end up looking exactly the same.

9. The evolution of social behaviour

Fear, aggression, submission and dominance determine the behaviour of social canids. These four mechanisms originated during evolution because they proved to be the best strategy at particular times. It is difficult to prove the advantages of being social, which means to exchange a certain and immediate advantage for a dubious future reward. Social behaviour may have evolved in various ways.

As we have mentioned briefly, the evolution of social behaviour in social insects happens according to kin selection, as Hamilton[22] emphasised.

In the honeybee, *Apis mellifera*, a worker is a sterile female. Her sisters are also workers, except for a few which will be fertile queens. It is the nutrition given to the grubs that causes some bees to become workers and others queens, although the potential to become fertile is a genetic feature. The evolution of this potential is an immediate advantage only for those who possess it. Kin selection must therefore be able to account for the evolution of this pattern.

Ants, *Formicidae*, bees, *Apidae*, wasps, *Vespoidea*, and termites, *Isoptera*, are all social insects with complex, organised societies. The first three of these belong to the order *hymenoptera* and Hamilton suggested that what enables them to develop social behaviour is their *haplodiploid* genetics. All hymenoptera males develop from unfertilised eggs and have only one set of chromosomes, i.e. they are haploid. All females develop from normal fertilised eggs and have two sets of chromosomes, i.e. they are diploid. Consequently, a female of a *haplodiploid* species has three-quarters of her genes in common with her sisters, but only half her genes in common with her daughters. In a normal diploid species, like humans, wolves, dogs and cats, she would have half her genes in common with both her sisters and her daughters.

Hence, it is more advantageous for a female hymenopteran to preserve her genes by nursing and protecting her sisters, than to start a family of her

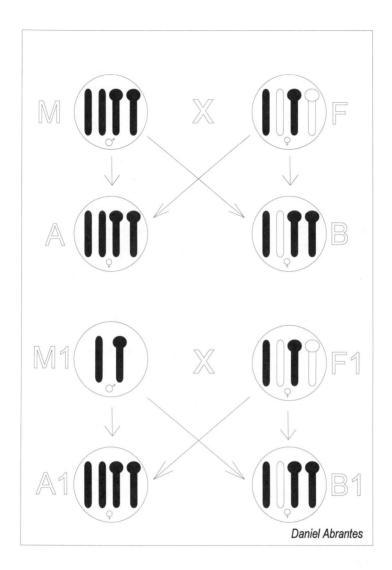

Daniel Abrantes

Reproduction in diploid and haplo-diploid species - In a normal diploid species like the dog, females A and B have exactly half of their genes in common with their mother F and their father M. Sisters A and B have also 50% genes in common.

In a haplo-diploid species, like the hymnoptera, females A1 and B1 have 50% of their genes in common with their mother F1, but among them they have in common all their father's (M1) genes, and 50% of their mother's (F2) genes. In all they have, thus, 75% common genes.

Illustration by Daniel Abrantes

own. In other words, she is more *in family* with her sisters than she ever will be with her offspring.

This genetic reward explains the social behaviour of the honeybee, but not all animals are haplodiploid and have such sophisticated genetics.

Kin selection also explains the evolution of the behaviour and genetics regulating both population density and the evolution of sex, as Maynard Smith indicated.[23] Both are relevant to our present study, as they account for the evolution of social behaviour in general and some patterns specifically.

To maintain a constant-sized population, each pair of animals must, on average, produce two offspring. A tiny deviation from this average for many generations invariably leads to a huge increase or decrease in numbers, with unpredictable consequences. Amazingly, most species maintain a population density which fluctuates between certain perimeters.

There are two ways to explain this: (1) the fertility of individuals rises or falls according to a rise or decline in the density of the population, or (2) the individual's chances of survival depend on the fluctuation of the population density.

Obviously, a huge growth in the population leads to starvation, which decimates it. Also, since such a population will not be so healthy, disease will prevail. It is, though, very seldom that a population increases to such an extent that starvation becomes an option to regulate it. This is due to special behavioural mechanisms evolved by *group selection*, as Wynne-Edwards[24] puts it. Such behaviour is advantageous to the group, and thus to the species, but not necessarily to the individual.

There are, however, some behaviour patterns which prevent excessive population growth that cannot be explained by means of traditional selection upon individuals, rather than on a group or a species.

We have seen that *territorial behaviour* has an aggression and fear limiting function, but in many species it also has a population density regulating effect. The establishment of territories may regulate, for example, a wolf population in a specific area. In most birds, a breeding pair occupies and claims a territory in which they collect food for their young. A male and a female wolf may stroll and hunt together, but will not normally breed unless they occupy a territory. The wolf pack territory is formed around hunting grounds and the den where cubs are born and spend their infancy. Such behaviour limits population growth because a wolf pack incapable of defending a territory from intruders is probably also incapable of breeding or maintaining their cubs. Aggression, and its regulation by natural selection, determines the size of the bird or wolf pack's territory. Excessively aggres-

Fear, aggression, submission and dominance determine the behaviour of social canids like the wolf and the domestic dog. These four mechanisms originated during evolution because they proved to be the best strategy at particular times.

sive animals, attempting to defend too large an area, are prone to injury and death and waste too much energy on skirmishes, meaning they are not providing for their young. Excessively shy or fearful animals do not succeed in establishing a territory, or may establish one too small to include an adequate supply of food for themselves and their progeny.

Ultimately, it is the need to establish and control a territory that triggers the evolution of social behaviour, at least in some species. This is yet another reason to develop submission and dominance. If an animal resolves inter-group conflicts with aggression and fear, it may be exhausted when subsequently compelled to expel an intruder from its territory. Thus the *alien* and *mate* strategy originated and evolved. It is impossible to fight everybody all the time, so a mate is confronted using energy saving procedures. Submission and dominance also control population density, since they rely on individual recognition. The number of personal recognitions an animal is capable of must have a limit. If this number exceeds a certain level it makes recognition inefficient, switching off the mate/alien strategy; fear/aggression displays then replace submission/dominance behaviour.

This is my view, but I would not claim that all social behaviour controls population density and growth. However, according to Wynne-Edwards the origin of all social behaviour lies in *epideictic* displays, whose function it is to provide information about population density.

Mice, *Murinae*, and domestic fowl, *Gallus gallus domesticus*, for example, are very susceptible to changes in population density. When numbers increase there is much wrestling and fighting. Mice may stop breeding, and lemmings, *Lemmus lemmus*, reportedly migrate. Individuals refrain from breeding to ensure the population does not exhaust its food supply according to the theory of group selection. This is not the only option. Running away or showing unreserved submission is often a better strategy for the individual, than to be killed or seriously injured. Submissive individuals nevertheless favour the survival of their group. Genetically speaking this is a difficult argument to defend.

We could say that animals only ever act in their own interests—never for the good of the group or the species. For the individual, all the others are just a bunch of bothersome competitors constantly exasperating one's life. Justifying the existence of genetically *altruistic* individuals is therefore a problem. How could a group come to consist *wholly* of altruistic individuals? In a *mixed* group, selection eliminates altruism: only those who do not restrain from breeding pass their genes to the next generation. In other words: dominant genes would prevail at the cost of the submissive ones. There are three possible answers.

(1) We can assume that if a population consists of many small groups, a wholly altruistic group can arise by chance. The groups could arise by a genetically determined tendency to refrain from breeding at high population densities. Difficulties arise, however, when accounting for the inhibition of interbreeding and how a small group infected by a selfish individual can get rid of its *non-altruistic* genes. The only way out, in my view, is if such a little group remains isolated forever. Finally, because of the lack of outcrossing, a new species will be formed—a totally altruistic species. Small populations are, however, troublesome from a genetic point of view.

The problem is that natural selection—interaction with the environment—is not the sole source of genetic variation. Gene frequencies may change by *genetic drift*, an occurrence especially likely in small populations. Obviously we know nothing about altruistic genes, or about other genes they

Learning how to become social animals—dog language is learned, by trial and error, at an early age by the sheer interaction with siblings, parents and other adults members of the pack.

probably connect with. It is, nevertheless, perfectly conceivable that some genes would simply *drift* from the original gene pool by not occurring in consecutive matings. Depending on species, this is again very likely in isolated small groups. All 1100 Przevalski's horses, *Equus Przevalskii*, in captivity today descend from 13 animals. Of the 26 genes carried by the original 13 animals, at any given locus of the chromosome, an average of 10.5 remain in the population today.[25]

The consequences of this are unpredictable, not least for our altruistic genes, jeopardising the whole theory. Mutations may also affect the gene pool, though usually only at very low rates. From a practical point of view, we need not fear the appearance of a sole mutant selfish gene in an altruistic population—only if it would largely enhance the fitness of the individual. Selection for fitness determines the gene pool of a certain population and mutant genes only enhance fitness if the environment also changes in their favour. Nonetheless, it must be said, mutations are the elements upon which selection operates.

It is unlikely that social behaviour evolved by means of small isolated altruistic groups. This line of thought may prove fruitful however, as we look at a third alternative to explain altruistic behaviour.

(2) The difference between altruism and selfishness may be a matter of *education* and not of genetics.[26] Education may spread altruism to all members of a group. As Maynard Smith stressed, this stipulates that all members of the species be *genetically educable*. It also implies the creation of some method of eliminating *genetically ineducable* individuals, in the event that they should arise by mutation. Herein may lie the foundation of the social behaviours we call dominance and submission and their genetic basis. Elimination of *ineducable individuals* is very likely to result from a genetically determined and instinctive intolerance of *non-conformisme*. In other words, those who do not contribute to the group and do not show submission are rejected. Selection then favours individuals with the best capacity for submission and since there must be an individual to submit to, the very existence of submission presupposes the existence of dominance. Ineducable individuals are also prone to fail because selfish beings are unlikely to care properly for their offspring, although this may be difficult to prove. It is improbable that selection can produce an organism complex enough to sacrifice itself for its progeny, but not for other members of the group. This would require each individual to reflect on the gene-mathematics of every action in every situation.

(3) Both previous explanations contain ideas which are highly unlikely. The fundamental problem is that a group consisting *wholly* of *altruistic individuals* is not a *stable strategy*. It is still vulnerable to the appearance of a selfish individual, for instance by mutation, in spite of them being *genetically educable individuals*. *Submission* is not stable and therefore needs an antagonist. The strategy *dominance* cannot be stable either, but as an antithesis to *submission*, it fulfils its role.

An *evolutionarily stable strategy*[27] or ESS, is as a strategy that is successful when competing with copies of itself. If a strategy is successful, then copies of it will tend to expand in the population and will eventually become almost universal. An ESS must be successful when compared with different strategies that might arise by mutation or invasion, as in the case of small, isolated populations of altruistic individuals. A strategy that is not *evolutionarily stable* does not last long in the world.

It is therefore perfectly conceivable that *dominance* and *submission* originated as an evolutionary necessity. They are probably the only viable options to establish an evolutionarily stable strategy for highly aggressive social animals. In their absence no complex society can exist for long, except in rare cases of haplodiploid organisms, such as hymenoptera. However, canids, being diploid, need to have genetic mapping to eventually develop dominance and submission behaviour. As we have seen, selection obviously worked towards a development of these behavioural traits, not at birth, but when the young begin interacting with other adult members of their pack. These adults are their relatives, and kin selection governs their behaviour. As long as wolves, African hunting dogs, coyotes and dogs continue behaving and caring for their progeny the way they do, this proves to be the *evolutionarily stable strategy* for diploid social canids.

10. Sexual behaviour

Among the various interactions between social animals, sexual behaviour is one of the most interesting, since it usually includes displays rich in ritualised behaviour. Sexual behaviour may therefore give us some insight into the evolution of social behaviour.

Sexual behaviours exist to accomplish copulation, i.e. the propagation of an animal's genetic information. To attain its goal, sexual behaviour must ensure that an individual:

(1) mates with a member of its own, and not of a related, species.

(2) mates, or increases the frequency with which it mates.

(3) mates with a specific partner rather than one chosen at random.

(1) As we have seen, the choice of potential mating partners in many species occurs as a secondary round of imprinting, after the learning of primary life-saving sign-stimuli has taken place.

(2) The selection of traits which increase an individual's chances to mate have a large impact on their repertoire of social displays. These traits must be effective, or a great deal of the genetic information of the organism will disappear.

Sexual behaviour is obviously a social interaction. Male and female must tolerate one another, without injuring or killing each other. This seems obvious, and yet many males mate at their peril. Courtship behaviour has evolved to elicit sexual motivation, rather than aggression from the partner.

Female spiders, *Araneae,* normally react to animals smaller than themselves by attacking and eating them. Consequently, male spiders are in danger of ending up as food rather than mating partners. Evolution therefore provided them with complex patterns of behaviour to avoid this unfortunate eventuality. One of these patterns is a characteristic way of vibrating the female's web. Similarly, the black-headed gull, *Larus ridibundus,* has an intricate courtship repertoire, including *pacifying behaviour*. They usually defend the territory next to their nest by threatening intruders with a typical posture: a lowered head with the beak pointing at the intruder. Many other birds threaten in a similar way. Pacifying a mate offers maximum contrast to a threat display. During one stage of courtship the two partners stand with their heads raised, their beaks pointing downwards, and their heads turned away.

Polygamy (where a male mates several females) is the main cause for the development of elaborated sexual behaviour. Polygamy is more common than *polyandry* (where a female mates with several males) because a female can only lay a limited number of eggs, or carry a limited amount of progeny inside her body. Males, however, can increase the number of their offspring by mating with as many females as is practically possible.

Dogs and wolves, *Canidae*, are carnivores, and in principle monogamous, so that both partners help feed the young. Since they are *social* carnivores, all members of the group help feed the young. Polygamy is common in ungulates, such as horses, *Equidae*, cattle, *Bovidae*, or deer, *Cervidae,* where the young depend either on their mother's milk or on plants they collect. There is little a male ungulate can do to increase its offspring's chances of survival. He can defend the harem and young from predators, but this is seldom a viable option to flight. Natural selection has therefore emphasised characteristics such as size, horns and antlers, which enhance the male ungulate's chances of mating with several females. In carnivores however, the difference in size or weaponry between male and female is minimal. In equines, *Equidae,* as the zebra, *Equus burchelli*, natural selection does not favour weaponry or body size, but interspecific aggression and a degree of co-operation among stallions. Male zebras eagerly defend their mares and foals against the attack of predators.

(3) The third aspect of sexual selection relates to the specific choice of partner and was described by Darwin in 1859.[27] The goal is to choose the best possible mate. A good mate is one that is (a) very fertile, and (b) good at increasing the chances of survival of his progeny (which carry 50 per cent of the female's genes). This is why most females show great discrimination when choosing males.

The mechanisms involved in choosing a partner also reflect what it means to be social, rather than aggressive or fearful. Even in species where partners only meet for a limited time to copulate, specific courtship behaviour has evolved. Most of this behaviour is ritualised. It is also very complex, more than would be expected in species with otherwise very simple behavioural repertoires. Courtship behaviour in social canids is well developed

A careful wolf watching out for strangers—the wolf pack territory is formed around hunting grounds and the den where cubs are born and spend their infancy.

and consists of multiple patterns. To appreciate the importance of sexual behaviour in canids we need to understand some fundamental mechanisms determining the behaviour of animals.

Darwin pointed out that although a male with striking sexual characters may be the first to find a mate, this will not increase the fitness of his genes, unless it also ensures that he will mate with a female equally fit as a parent. The same applies to females, who need to select males fit as parents, and not only for their masculine features. In other words, in a monogamous species, secondary sexual characteristics, such as 'masculinity', are only favoured by selection if (a) they appear in individuals fitter than the average as parents, and (b) those individuals are able to find mates that are as fit as parents.

In Darwin's view, an association between *secondary sexual characteristics* and *fitness as parent* must exist, since both characterise the healthiest individuals in a population.

There is no proof that female canids choose their partners on the basis of secondary sexual characteristics, such as body size or ferocity, or the lack of

Drosophilidae, commonly called fruit flies, have been exceptionally useful in scientific research. Their short reproductive cycle (a new generation of adults develops in only two weeks) and uncomplicated genetics make them ideal subjects for studies of heredity.

it. However, there is a tendency towards a choice based on rank.[29] Generally, alpha females choose alpha males and vice-versa. There is also a tendency towards monogamy, even though this is not as rigid as in other species, such as jackals, *Canis aureus, adustus and mesomelas*.

Darwin's assumption is difficult to prove. Secondary traits, responsible for the selection of partners, must somehow increase the progeny of the individuals showing those traits. This is virtually impossible to confirm by means of field observations.

However, observations on laboratory populations of the fruit fly, *Drosophila subobscura*, have confirmed both the above facts, and enabled us to discover how females make their choice of mate.[30]

Male fruit flies are polygamous, while females are monogamous. Females store sperm after mating and discharge it to fertilise each egg as it suits them. An old female may continue to lay unfertilised eggs because she no longer carries any sperm, and yet refuses to mate again.

Two groups of females, similar in genetic constitution, were mated to either outbred or inbred males. The total number of eggs laid by females of the two groups was about the same, but the proportion of eggs that hatched was not. Females mated by outbred males laid an average of four times more hatching eggs than the other females. Inbred males produced fewer sperm than the outbred males and some of it was defective. Outbred males were better parents in that they were more fertile, but the females obviously did not know this.

The outbred males' fertility combined with the monogamy of the females resulted in about four times as many offspring, as in those which mated with inbred males. We can therefore conclude that there should be a strong natural selection in favour of outbred males and females that choose them as partners.

A subsequent experiment showed that encounters between virgin females and outbred males resulted in 90 per cent of matings, while encounters with inbred males led to matings in only about 50 per cent of cases. It was not because inbred males did not try, for they courted continuously and made repeated attempts to mount unwilling females. Why was there such a difference in the proportion of matings in the two cases?

The courtship behaviour of fruit flies is very specific. The male approaches the female with quick flicks of his wings. He then strokes her with his front legs and circles around until he faces her with his mouth extended towards her. The female then begins a very quick side-stepping dance, moving to one side and then to the other. The male follows her, side-stepping and trying to maintain eye contact. Suddenly the female stands still and the male must be swift enough to circle round and rapidly mount her. If the male leaves this even a fraction of a second too late, the whole process needs to begin again.

Sometimes, a female may stop in the middle of the side-stepping dance and simply fly away. From the first approach of the male to the actual mounting, the whole display takes only a few seconds, but then fruit flies probably have a different notion of time than us.

The difference is that with outbred males mating usually occurs after one or two dances. With an inbred male, a whole series of dances usually takes place, and often the female flies away before the male mounts her. After a series of cold shoulders the inbred male becomes increasingly inpatient and approximates the female from the side or from behind, which is no way to conduct yourself if you are a male fruit fly courting a virgin female. Without side-step dancing the female will not allow him to mount her and his chances of a successful mating are zero.

The secret to success in courting a female fruit fly lies in keeping pace with her during the dance. An outbred male usually manages to keep visual contact with the female, while inbred males often fail to keep up. Females seem only to accept males that have been facing them while they execute their dance—maybe they find the co-ordination of movements with one another especially fascinating, who knows!

It is the greater physical fitness of outbred males that causes the differences in the males' behaviour. Outbred males are much more persistent. The females' criterion in choosing a mate is by selecting a good dancer and a great athlete. As a side effect, they get fertile mates too, not only producing more sperm, but also of a better quality than that of less athletic males.

Natural selection not only favours good dancers among males, but also

Courtship behaviour shows the patterns that natural selection has favoured. The goal is to ensure that the best male is mated with the best female. The mechanisms of dominace and submission may have evolved as secondary sexual traits.

females insisting on the dancing ritual before mating. They are favoured above their sisters. Females which do not execute the side-stepping dance at all, or allow bad-dancers to mount them, tend to mate with less fertile males leaving four times less progeny.

Using these experiments, Dobzhansky[31] proved that the laws of genetics are compatible with Darwin's natural selection. The Darwinian concept of sexual selection explains the evolution of the courtship dance ritual if, and only if, males with characteristics which increase their mating success are also fitter as parents. Such a correlation may well exist because, '... both will be features of the most vigorous members of the population,'[32] in Darwin's words.

The behaviour of *Drosophila subobscura* is a clear example that the structures of ritualised behaviour are extremely complex, especially considering that fruit flies are not complicated animals. There can be no doubt that in higher animals such as mammals, selection aiming at guaranteeing that an individual shall choose *one* mate among many of its conspecifics, can account for the development of secondary sexual characters.

Although there is no side-step dancing in the courtship ritual of social canids, many general elements of fruit fly behaviour do apply. Most striking is the resemblance among the females who do not allow males to mount them without a preliminary ritualised approach. This behaviour is obviously so intrinsic from a genetic point of view, that it is similar in domestic dogs and wolves.

Female dogs choose partners through elaborated rituals. Normally, they reject their initial approaches and whenever the male becomes pushy the female answers with aggressive behaviour. Females are in heat for a considerable amount of time, and yet they will only allow a male to mount them during a relatively short interval. This may be to ensure that only one male, the fittest, fertilises her eggs. When so much attention is given to courtship behaviour, it is unlikely that several males may gain her attention.

Courtship behaviour allows a female wolf to unwittingly check the paternal abilities of her potential mate. This is of great importance for a female because she is investing a vast amount of energy in the pregnancy. She cannot afford to make mistakes. Male wolves also invest a lot, as they usually stay with the females and help them rear the cubs.

In other species, such as domestic dogs, however, males will usually mate as many females as they can. This may be due to a *genetic drift*—the monogamous genes just drifted away in male dogs—although this is unlikely. More probable is the influence of social context.

*There is no proof that
female canids choose
their partners on the
basis of secondary sexual
characteristics, such as
body size or ferocity, or
the lack of it. However,
there is a tendency
towards a choice based
on rank. Generally, alpha
females choose alpha
males and vice-versa.
There is also a tendency
towards monogamy, even
though this is not as rigid
as in other species, such
as jackals.*

A female wolf's courtship behaviour confirms Darwin's view. She not only gets the most fertile male of all—since he is the alpha male he is usually the healthiest—she is probably getting the best parent, too.

Moreover, whenever the female chooses the alpha male, selection also favours other features. To be the alpha, a wolf has to show particular behaviours to maintain its rank with the least possible waste of energy. This means mastering the mechanisms of dominance and submission. Thus dominance and submission behaviours become secondary sexual characteristics which females favour.

In courtship behaviour we are able to observe many elements of dominance and submission as well as juvenile and parental behaviour. Male and female successively submit and dominate one another. They play *the cub role* in succession and if everything is satisfactory, they will mate and have progeny of their own. This offspring will give their social genes to the next generation and so on for as long as natural selection will favour those individuals with those specific characteristics.

This is one point where our selection of breeding animals in domestic dogs can prove detrimental. We choose the sire and dam according to certain aesthetic standards, or learned patterns of behaviour. We never test our dogs for their parental abilities, the ability to provide for their progeny, or how good they are at performing the rituals that natural selection originally favoured. If these abilities were the cause of secondary sexual traits, as for instance the ability to show dominance and submission, we are indeed selecting incorrectly.

Wolves may howl to find a lost partner. An alpha males howls mainly to locate the alpha female or the cubs. Howling also plays a social role in the life of the pack and wolves will often howl before going hunting.

11. A question of conformity

There is great confusion over the use of the terms dominance and submission. Some modern *animal behaviourists* combine them at random: dominance aggression, fear aggression, predatory aggression, submissive aggression, territorial aggression, etc.

Such behaviour patterns are not necessarily motivated by these drives. It is not, for example, possible to be fearful and aggressive and the same time. Fear leads to passivity or flight, and aggression to attack. One cannot be immobile and attack simultaneously, or attack under flight. When people speak of fear-aggression they mean submissive-aggression, which may occur when an aggressor does not accept the animal's submission and there is no possibility of escape. The initial submission turns into submission and fear, and finally into submission and aggression. When a dog attacks another it is *always* aggressive.

The idea of dominance-aggression is biased as well. It is possible to be aggressive and dominant, but the term suggests the dog attacks because it is dominant. This is not true. No dog attacks because of dominance as this would be contradictory. Dominance aims at *controlling* another by means of *ritualised behaviour,* without harming or injuring it. The final attack, if there is one, is motivated by aggression alone.

The classification of dog behaviour in such categories was initially used by animal behaviourists, with a background in the veterinary profession. They used the terminology of their field in an attempt to apply systematic methods to companion animal behaviour. Ethology is not an exact science, in the same degree as fundamental biology, and yet it uses many of its scientific methods.

However, it is my opinion that this classification of dog behaviour is meaningless and damaging. For instance, saying that a dog is a fear-biter, i.e. shows fear-aggression, is equivalent to saying that the dog does not behave purposefully and is showing pathological behaviour. By rephrasing the verdict and saying that the dog shows *submissive-aggression* we simultaneously answer the question of how to solve the problem. The dog is submis-

The pack—wolves live in a world where energy is necessary for survival and where waste is heavy penalised. Only the fittest will survive long enough to give their genes to their offspring.

sive, which means reacting to a threat by another, giving in, surrendering. It only becomes aggressive because its behaviour does not have the desired effect. The dog is then under threat and ready to react by flight or immobility. If flight is not possible, it may freeze. Some do and die. Others resort to their last defence, they attack, and then the drive of aggression takes over. This situation is easily avoided by accepting the dog's submission or allowing it to flee.

Eventually, the young social predator masters the use of the four main mechanisms, their sign-stimuli and behavioural displays, combined with a rich variety of expressions. They are masters of the mechanisms that prevent them wasting time or energy in unnecessary displays. Social predators live in a world where energy is necessary for survival and where waste is heavy penalised. Only the fittest will survive long enough to give their genes to their offspring. Among these highly aggressive social predators the fittest are undoubtedly the best in using the mechanisms of dominance and submission, and their offspring will be even better at using them.

12. Conclusion

1. *Motivation* is what compels an animal to do what it does.

2. A *drive* is a force, an urge onward, a basic need, a compulsive energy.

3. *Fear* is the drive that motivates the individual to react to an incoming threat.

    3.1. A *threat* is everything that may harm, inflict pain or injury to the individual, or decreases its chances of survival.

    3.2. *Fear* elicits flight, immobility or distress behaviour.

4. *Aggression* is a drive directed towards the elimination of competition.

    4.1. Fighting involves risk. Evolution has developed mechanisms to restrain the intensity of aggressive behaviour. One of these mechanisms is a genetically programmed tendency to establish *territories*.

    4.2. The *ritualisation* of aggressive behaviour is another genetically programmed restraint during conflict.

        4.2.1. A *hierarchy* or a *rank-order* is a dominance-submission relationship established and maintained by means of ritualised behaviour. Its structure depends on: (1) species, (2) individuals, (3) available resources, (4) the constitution of the group, and (5) the environment.

5. *Dominance-submission* relations limit the use of aggression or fear, thus diminishing conflicts that might decrease the individual's chances of survival.

    5.1. Dominance and submission originated as an evolutionary necessity. They establish an *evolutionarily stable strategy* for highly aggressive social animals.

5.2. Dominance and submission behaviours evolved partially as *secondary sexual characters.*

5.3. *Dominance,* or *social-aggression,* is a drive directed towards the elimination of competition from a mate.

5.3.1. *Mates* are two or more animals who live closely together and depend on one another for survival.

5.3.2. *Aliens* are two animals who do not live closely together and do not depend on one another for survival.

5.3.3. *Social-aggression* usually elicits ritualised aggressive behaviour, where a mate is not injured. It may consist of body postures, facial and vocal expressions.

5.4. *Submission,* or *social-fear*, is the drive that motivates the individual to react to an incoming *social-threat* from a mate.

5.4.1. A *social-threat* is everything that may cause submissive behaviour or flight, without the individual being harmed.

5.4.2. *Social-fear* usually elicits submissive behaviour following the mate's threat or flight. It may also elicit vocal distress or displacement activity.

Barely 14,000 years ago we were predators on a par with our soul brother, the wolf.

The basis of social behaviour in canids -

3.2 shows a neutral expression.

From 3. to 1. there is an increase in dominance and from 3. to 6. an increase in submission.

From .2 to .0 there is an increase in aggression and from .2 to .4 an increase in fear.

Displays .2 show dominance and submission without aggression or fear.

Display 1.1. is the alpha wolf and 3.3. shows a greeting ceremony, a ritualised aggression and fear behaviour showing slight traces of dominance and submission.

Empty spaces, such as 2.0 and 3.0, have never been observed.

13. Final note

The cells of an organism transform energy, maintain their identity, and reproduce. A life form is dependent on many thousands of simultaneous and precisely regulated metabolic reactions to support them. Specific cell enzymes control each of these reactions and their co-ordination with numerous other reactions in the organism—this applies to all life, from single-celled algae to human beings!

Barely 14,000 years ago we were predators on a par with our soul brother, the wolf. We too are highly aggressive animals, with sophisticated rituals and inhibition mechanisms—the most peculiar and refined of all being language.

Recent discoveries uncovered that the learning of human language is partially a kind of imprinting. Three-day-old babies recognise consonants as sign-stimuli and can discriminate between sounds in their own language and those of foreign ones. Maybe human and animal behaviour are two sides of the same evolutionary coin after all.

Table - Behaviour in solitary and social canids.

Drive	Goal	Process	Releaser	Means	Organism		
					Solitary predator	Social predator	
						Alien	Mate
Self-preservation	Transform energy Maintain identity	Digestion Defence Competition	Hunger Danger Aggression	Fear Attack	Predating Flight -	- Flight Attack	- Submission Dominance
Reproduction	Replication	Sexuality	Chemical	Courtship	Copulation	-	Courtship Dominance/submission

Notes

1. The American Heritage Concise Dictionary, *Houghton Mifflin Company 1994.*
The Oxford Thesaurus, *Oxford University Press, 1991.*
2. Darwin, C. (1859) On The Origin Of Species By Means Of Natural Selection, Or The Preservation Of Favoured Races In The Struggle For Life; — (1872) The Expression Of The Emotions in Man and Animals.
3. Watson, J. B. (1924) Behaviorism, New York, *The Norton Library*.
Skinner, B. F. (1938) The Behaviorism of Organisms, *New York, Appleton-Century-Crofts.*
4. Pavlov, I. (1927) Conditioned Reflexes.
5. Lorenz, K. (1965) Evolution and Modification of Behaviour, *The Univ. of Chicago Press.*
—The Foundations of Ethology, *New York, Springer-Verlag.* (1981).
Tinbergen, N. (1951) The Study of Instinct, *Oxford Univ. Press.*
Frisch, K. von. (1965) Tanzsprache und Orientierung der Bienen, *Heidelberg, Springer Verlag.*
6. Lorenz, K. (1963) Das Sogennante Böse (On Aggression), *Wien, Borotha-Scöler Verlag.*
7. Maynard Smith, J. (1958) The Theory of Evolution, *Penguin Books England.*
Dawkins, R. (1976) The Selfish Gene, *Oxford Univ. Press.*
8. Peirce, C. S. (1958) Selected Writings, *London, Constable and Co.*
9. The American Heritage Concise Dictionary, Houghton Mifflin Company 1994.
The Oxford Thesaurus, Oxford University Press 1991.
Microsoft Encarta 1994, Microsoft Corporation and Funk & Wagnall's Corporation.
10. Christiansen, F. W. & Rothausen, B. (1983) Behaviour Patterns Inside and Around The Den Of A Captive Wolf Pack, *Lungholm Wolf Research Station, Denmark.*
11. The American Heritage Concise Dictionary, Houghton Mifflin Company 1994.
The Oxford Thesaurus, Oxford University Press 1991.
Microsoft Encarta 1994, Microsoft Corporation and Funk & Wagnall's Corporation.

12. Lorenz, K. (1963) *op. cit.*
13. Hamilton, W. D. (1964) The Genetical Theory of Natural Selection, *J. Theoretical Biology 7, (1)1-16, (2) 17-32.*
14. Wynne-Edwards, V.C. (1962) Animal Dispersion In Relation To Social Behaviour, *Edinburgh, Oliver & Boyd.*
15. Hamilton, W. D. (1964) *op. cit.* Dawkins, R. (1976), *op. cit.*
16. Christiansen, F. W. & Rothausen, B. (1983) *op. cit.*
17. The American Heritage Concise Dictionary, Houghton Mifflin Company 1994.
The Oxford Thesaurus, Oxford University Press 1991.
Microsoft Encarta 1994, Microsoft Corporation and Funk & Wagnall's Corporation.
18. Lorenz, K. (1963), *op. cit.*
19. Mech, L.D. (1970) The Wolf: The Ecology And Behavior Of An Endangered Species, *New York, The Natural History Press.*
20. Zimen, E. (1981) The Wolf, Its Place In The Natural World, *Souvenir Press.*
21. Dawkins, R., *op. cit.*
22. Hamilton, W.D. *op. cit.*
23. Maynard-Smith, J., (1958), *op. cit.*
24. Wynne-Edwards, V.C. (1962) *op. cit.*
25. Ryder, O. (1993), Przevalski's horse: prospects for reintroduction into the wild, *Conservation Biology 7-1993: 13-15.*
26. Maynard-Smith, J., *op. cit.*
27. Maynard Smith, J. (1974) The Theory of Games And The Evolution Of Animal Conflicts, *Journal of Theor. Biology, 47, 209-221.*
28. Darwin, C. (1859) *op. cit.*
29. Mech, L.D., *op. cit.*
    Zimen, E. (1981), *op. cit..*
30. Dobzhansky, T. (1951) Genetics And The Origin Of Species, *New York, Columbia University Press.*
31. Dobzhansky, T. (1951) *op. cit.*
32. Darwin, C. (1859) *op. cit*

Litterature

Ethology, Biologi and Zoology

Abrantes, R.A., (1986) - The Expression of Emotions in Man and Canid (Waltham Symposium, Cambridge University).
Abrantes, R.A., (1993) - The Develpoment of Social Behaviour (in The Behaviour of Dogs and Cats, by members of the APBC).
Abrantes, R.A., (1994) - The Art and Science of Communication (in Transcript of Waltham APBC Symposiun 1994).

Christiansen, F.W & Rothausen, B., (1983) - Behaviour Patterns Inside and Around the Den of a Captive Wolf Pack.

Darwin, C., (1859) - The Origin of Species.
Darwin, C., (1872) - The Expression of the Emotions in Man and Animals.
Darwin, C., (1978) - The Voyage of Charles Darwin, edited by C. Ralling.
Dawkins, R., (1976) - The Selfish Gene.
Dawkins, R., (1982) - The extended phenotype.
Dawkins, R., (1986) - The Blind Watchmaker.
Dawkins, M.S., (1986) - Unravelling Animal Behaviour.
De Waal, F., (1982) -Chimpanzee Politics—Power and Sex Among Apes.

Fox, M.W., (1968) - Aggression Its Adaptive and Maladaptive Significance in Man and Animals.
Fox. M.W., (1971) - Overview and Critique of Stages and Periods in Canine Development.
Fox, M.W., (1972)- Socio-Ecological Implications of individual Differences in Wolf Litters: A Developmental and Evolutionary Perspective.
Fox, M.W., (1972) - The Social Significance of Genital Licking in the Wolf, Canis Lupus.
Fox, M.W., (1972) - Social Dynamics of Three Captive Wolf Packs.
Fox, M.W., (1973) - Physiological and Biochemical Correlates of Individual Differences in Behaviour of the Wolf.

Gubernick, D.J., Klopfer, P.H., (1981) - Parental Care in Mammals.

Hess, E.H., (1973) - Imprinting.

Lorenz, K., (1963) - Das sogenannte Böse.
Lorenz, K., (1965) - Evolution and Modification of Behavior.
Lorenz, K., (1973) - Die Rückseite des Spiegels.
Lorenz, K., (1981) - The Foundations of Ethology.
Lorenz, K., (1983) - Nedbrydningen af det menneskelige.

Maynard Smith, J. (1958) - The Theory of Evolution.
Maynard Smith, J. (1974) - The Theory of Games And The Evolution Of Animal Conflicts, *Journal of Theor. Biology, 47, 209-221.*
Mech, D., (1970) - The Wolf.
Mech, D., (1988) - The Arctic Wolf: Living with the Pack.

Ploog, D.W., (1966) - Biological Bases for Instinct and Behaviour: Studies on the Development of Social Behaviour in Squirrel Monkeys.'

Rees, L. (1984) - The Horse' mind.

Smith, J.M., (1958) - The Theory of Evolution.
Simonsen, H.B. (1985) - Hestens adfærd.

Tinbergen, N., (1953) - Social Behavior in Animals.

Van Hooff, J.A.R.A.M., (1966) - The Facial Displays of Catarrhine Monkeys and Apes.

Wickler, W., (1967) - Socio-Sexual Signals and Their Intraspecific Imitation among Primates.
Wynne-Edwards, V.C. (1962) - Animal Dispersion In Relation To Social Behaviour, *Edinburgh, Oliver & Boyd.*

Zimen, E., (1981) - The Wolf - his Place in the Natural World.

Canine Behaviour

Abrantes, R.A., (1983) - Enquiry into the Effectiveness of Human-Dog Communication (IEMT, Wien).
Abrantes, R.A., (1987) - Hundesprog.
Abrantes, R.A., (1997) - Dog Language—An Encyclopedia Of Canine Behaviour.

Dunbar, I., (1979 - Dog Behavior - Why Dogs Do What They Do.

Fox, M.W., (1971) - Behaviour of Wolfes, Dogs and Related Canids.
Fox, M.W., (1975) - The Wild Canids.
Fox, M.W., (1978) - Man, Wolf and Dog.

Trumler, E., (1971) - Mit dem Hund auf Du.

Hart, B.L., (1980) - Canine Behavior.
Kruuk, H., (1972) - The Spottes Hyena - A Study of Predation and Social Behavior.

Van Larwick-Goodall, H.J., (1970) - Uskyldige Dræbere.

Genetics

Abrantes, R., Hallgren, A. (1982) - On the Testing of Behavioural Traits.
Dobzhansky, T. (1951) - Genetics And The Origin Of Species, *New York, Columbia University Press.*
Hamilton, W. D. (1964) - The Genetical Evolution Of Social Behavior. I.II. J. Theoret. Biol. 7:1-52.
Jones, S., (1993) - The Language of the Genes.
Scott, J.P., Fuller, J.L., (1965) - Genetics and the Social Behaviour of the Dog.

Psychology

Skinner, B.F., (1938) - The Behavior of Organisms.
Skinner, B.F., (1974) - About Behaviorism.
Watson, J.B., (1930) - Behaviorism.

Epistemology

Peirce, C. S. (1958) Selected Writings, *London, Constable and Co.*
Popper, K.R., (1962) - The Logic of Scientific Discovery.
Popper, K.R., (1972) - Objective Knowledge.
Quine, W.v.O., (1961) - From a logical point of vue.
Schlick, M., (1949) - Philosophy of Nature.

Roger Abrantes, ethologist, cand. art. DHC, DF, MAPBC, is the author to 15 books published in Danish, Swedish, Norwegian and English. He is currently the scientific director of the Institute of Ethology at the Høng Agriculture School, Denmark.

RA has participated in many TV and radio programmes all over the world. He has been adviser for the Danish Police Force, Technologic Institute, the Icelandic Kennel Club and guest lecturer at the Danish Veterinary University. He is in high demand as a speaker at international symposiums in Europe and America. He often guest lectures at several universities, including the University of Illinois in the USA.

You can order books by calling or writing to

Wakan Tanka Publishers
11 South 706, Lillian Court, Naperville, Il. 60564, USA
Phone and telefax (+1) 630 904 0895
E-mail <WTanka@aol.com>
http://users.aol.com/jemeyers/wt.htm

Wakan Tanka Seminars
arranges talks and seminars with the author of this book. Please call for more information.

You can also contact the author of this book at
<abrantes@vip.cybercity.dk>

Association Of Pet Behaviour Councellors
PO Box 46, Worcester, WR8 9YS, England

Tel/Fax +44 1386 751151
E-mail <apbc@petbcent.demon.co.uk>
http://webzone1.co.uk/www/apbc

Dog Language

An Encyclopedia Of Canine Behaviour
by Roger Abrantes

Dog Language tells us why dogs do what they do and how we can express ourselves so that our dogs understand us better. It is a systematic book, ordered alphabetically with 293 entries and 94 beautiful drawings illustrating over 150 different dog expressions.

First published in Scandinavia in 1986 as *'Hundesprog'*, this book became a great success and has since then helped many thousands of dog owners, instructors, behaviour students and veterinarians to understand dogs. Now available in English, the present edition of *Dog Language* is an updated, highly revised and enlarged version of the original *'Hundesprog'*.

Following the traditions of the school of ethology founded by Konrad Lorenz, *Dog Language* is based on many hours of research, observation and study. *Dog Language* is a no-nonsense book, written in a modern and uncomplicated style—a book for all readers with interest in dogs, wolves and other canids.